# Now and then
# Journeys

Monica Hughes

Heinemann
LIBRARY

**www.heinemann.co.uk/library**
Visit our website to find out more information about **Heinemann Library** books.

To order:
☎ Phone 44 (0) 1865 888066
▤ Send a fax to 44 (0) 1865 314091
▭ Visit the Heinemann Bookshop at www.heinemann.co.uk/library to browse our
catalogue and order online.

First published in Great Britain by Heinemann
Library, Halley Court, Jordan Hill, Oxford
OX2 8EJ, part of Harcourt Education.
Heinemann is a registered trademark of Harcourt
Education Ltd.

Editorial: Sarah Eason and Georga Godwin
Design: Jo Hinton-Malivoire and Tokay,
    Bicester, UK (www.tokay.co.uk)
Picture Research: Rosie Garai and
    Debra Weatherley
Production: Edward Moore

Originated by Dot Gradations Ltd
Printed and bound in China by South China
Printing Company

ISBN 0 431 18645 6 (hardback)
07 06 05 04 03
10 9 8 7 6 5 4 3 2 1

ISBN 0 431 18650 2  (paperback)
07 06 05 04 03
10 9 8 7 6 5 4 3 2 1

**British Library Cataloguing in Publication Data**
Hughes, Monica
Now and Then – Journeys
388'.09
A full catalogue record for this book is available
from the British Library.

**Acknowledgements**
The Publishers would like to thank the following
for permission to reproduce photographs:
Alamy Images **p. 12**; Alvey & Towers **pp. 6**, **14**,
**16**; Corbis/E. O. Hoppé **p. 5**; Corbis/Hulton-
Deutsch Collection **pp. 9**, **17**; Corbis/Roger
Ressmeyer **p. 22**; Francis Frith Collection **p. 13**;
Mary Evans Picture Library/Henry Grant **p. 7**;
Nasa **p. 23**; Newscast **p. 20**; Paul Amos **p. 18**;
Peter Evans **p. 8**; Popperfoto **pp. 11**, **15**, **21**;
Popperfoto/Alamy **p. 19**; Stockfile/Steve Behr
**p. 4**; Trip/M. Jenkin **p. 10**.

Cover photograph reproduced with permission
of Getty Images/Hulton Archive.

The Publishers would like to thank Annie Davy
for her assistance in the preparation of this book.

Every effort has been made to contact copyright
holders of any material reproduced in this book.
Any omissions will be rectified in subsequent
printings if notice is given to the Publishers.

# Contents

# Bikes

Now it's **fun** to go out on a bike.

4

Then

It was **hard** delivering things by bike.

Most cars were the same shape and colour.

Then

# Buses

Now

Glasgow Buchanan Bus Stn 240

ALL DAY TRAVEL | UNLIMITED £1.95

First

MD73

R305 GHS

Who gives out the tickets on a bus like this?

The conductor gave out the tickets and the inspector checked them on this bus.

Then

# Trams

Trams like this are very
special and quite rare today.

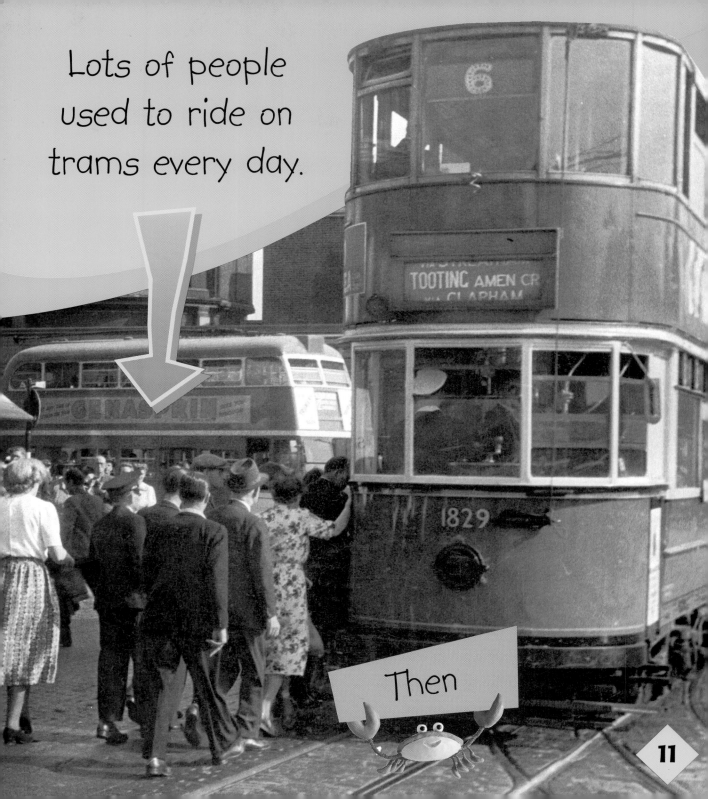

# Lorries

Have you seen a lorry as **big** as this?

Now

LONG VEHICLE

12

Then

At one time lorries were much smaller.

# Trains

Now

This train goes very **quickly** and is **quiet** and clean.

# Barges

Now people mainly use barges for their holidays.

Then

Barges were used to carry **heavy** loads from place to place.

# Ships

Now people use ships
to go on short journeys.

Very **large** ships took people on long journeys.

Then

# Planes

Now

Large planes take lots of people on long journeys very **quickly**.

This plane is much smaller.

Then

# Space travel

Now people can live and work in space.

# Index

The end

## Notes for adults

This series supports the child's knowledge and understanding of their world, in particular their personal, social and emotional development. The following Early Learning Goals are relevant to the series:

• make connections between different parts of their life experience
• show an awareness of change
• begin to differentiate between past and present
• introduce language that enables them to talk about their experiences in greater depth and detail.

It is important to relate the **Now** photographs to the child's own experiences and so help them differentiate between the past and present. The **Then** photographs can be introduced by using phrases like: *When I was your age, When granddad was a boy, Before you were born*. By comparing the two photographs they can begin to identify similarities and differences between the present and the past. Ask open-ended questions like: Do you remember when …? What might it be like …? What do you think …? This will help the child to develop their own ideas and extend their thinking.

Some of the methods of transport shown in the **Then** photographs will be familiar to the child, for example the car and the bus, encourage the child to identify differences. Other methods of transport that were once very common, like barges and trams, may be unfamiliar to the child. Travel by plane is now very common whereas travel by ship is more unusual. The child might also think about any aspects of the **Then** photographs that are more attractive, for example steam trains.

A follow up activity could involve doing pairs of **Then/Now** drawings of different kinds of vehicles. They could also visit a transport museum or vintage car rally and see real-life examples of past vehicles.